PIPELINES OF PROGRESS

AN UPDATE ON THE GLASS CEILING INITIATIVE

U.S. Department of Labor
Lynn Martin, Secretary
August, 1992

ISBN 0-16-038019-7

For sale by the U.S. Government Printing Office
Superintendent of Documents, Mail Stop: SSOP, Washington, DC 20402-9328
ISBN 0-16-038019-7

TABLE OF CONTENTS

FOREWORD

America is at a crossroad. Over fifty percent of its workforce is made up of minorities and women, yet it appears that their advancement is oftentimes hindered by artificial barriers -- glass ceilings. Can we afford, in today's global competition, to fail to make full use of the talent of all of our workers? Of course not.

When the Department of Labor, one year ago, released the report on its Glass Ceiling Initiative, it did so with its eyes on the future. At that time, we stated unequivocally that "the symptoms of this problem are manifest. Qualified minorities and women are all too often on the outside looking into the executive suite."

"Pipelines of Progress" is a look at what has occurred and is occurring, in America to ensure that artificial barriers are broken so that merit can determine the career advancement of talented minorities and women.

The basic message of this report is simple: While progress has been made in the workplace by minorities and women, the commitment and actions that led to this progress must be maintained and enhanced if the goal of full and equal employment opportunity is to be realized.

Over the past year the Department has made a strong and continued commitment to use its available tools and resources to remove glass ceiling barriers. We have done this because it is our responsibility under the law, and because it is the right thing to do.

We have prevailed upon employers to give this issue their personal attention. Our Office of Federal Contract Compliance Programs (OFCCP) has provided more than 25,000 hours of compliance assistance to those employers holding Federal Government contracts. That Office has initiated a new round of glass ceiling investigations using the knowledge and expertise gained from the pilot reviews of last year. We further continue to monitor the progress of the companies reviewed last year through progress reports and follow-up visits. Over 50,000 copies of "The Report on the Glass Ceiling Initiative" have been requested and distributed nationwide. Our Women's Bureau has organized and led discussions, conferences and public forums with senior managers and corporate executives from across the country.

This is the simple fact: few companies can afford glass ceilings. In a global marketplace that grows increasingly more competitive, companies need to promote the best people, regardless of race, gender, color or national origin.

Our pro-active outreach efforts reaffirm my belief that the '90s must be the decade of dialogue and action. There must be frank, honest discussion between employers and employees on career goals and on the expectations of employees and managers. There must also be open exchange between the Federal Government and those who fall within its mandates.

"Pipelines of Progress" does not mean that America's workplaces are free of discrimination. Much remains to be done by our business community, in unions, and in the public sector. The report does show what is actually being done this week, this month, this year, to change attitudes, perceptions and biases.

The Bush Administration and the Labor Department remain more than ever committed to shattering the glass ceiling. As we continue to look at the Fortune 500 world, we must begin to reach out to small and medium-sized employers. We can create networks of communication so that all employers can better manage and fully use the talents of America's diverse workforce. These actions are at the core of our obligation to ensure that America's working women and men remain the world's most productive and competitive workforce.

LYNN MARTIN
SECRETARY OF LABOR

Executive Summary

This report is largely focused on the steps companies can take and have taken to remove glass ceiling barriers. The companies discussed are those which have been subject to the Department's glass ceiling reviews as either part of the pilot reviews of last year, or as part of the ongoing reviews the Department now conducts. We believe this discussion should assist the entire corporate community, as individual companies identify their own glass ceiling barriers and implement strategies to remove them.

This report is also a good news, bad news document. The good news is that the participation rates of minorities and women in corporate management has improved. The bad news is that surveys in the corporate world do not point to an optimistic future unless commitments to positive change are sustained and enhanced. This report abounds with anecdotal evidence showing that glass ceiling barriers can be removed. It also demonstrates that the Department's enforcement effort must continue to be a critical component of the strategy to remove such barriers. But the report also underscores the fact that the challenge to shatter the glass ceiling takes far more time and effort than even the strongest of commitments can produce in one year.

I.   Workforce Trends

Research data on workplace advancement has yielded mixed results. It is encouraging to note that there is an increased awareness of the issue of diversity in corporate America. The key to real progress in attaining this goal, however, still remains at the pipeline levels of advancement, well below senior level management.

A Business Week survey released this year of 400 female managers found that almost half of the respondents believed that large companies have done "somewhat better" over the last five years in terms of hiring and promoting women executives. More than half of these same respondents also believed that the rate of progress has slowed down. Seventy percent of those female managers polled believed that the male-dominated corporate culture was an obstacle to their success (up from 60 percent two years ago).

A recent study of career progressions of over 1000 male and female managers in 20 Fortune 500 companies by researchers at Loyola University of Chicago and the Kellogg Graduate School of Management found that while these two groups were alike in almost every way, the "women with equal or better educations earn less on average than men and there are proportionately fewer women in top management positions."

The Department's own analysis of data filed by those companies holding Federal contracts does show, however, that minorities and women have made progress over the past 10 years. The proportion of corporate officials and managers who are minorities and women significantly increased during this time period.

II.   Corporate Management Reviews

During the past year, the Department has been monitoring the progress of the companies reviewed in the first round of pilot reviews through progress reports and follow-up visits.

The first round of reviews found that many of the Federal contractors believed they were in compliance, but when reviewed were found not to be. As a corrective measure, not only did the Department require progress reports, but it also conducted follow-up visits to substantiate the progress.

Some specific examples of the positive effects from the reviews and follow-up include:

*   **Commitment Continues at the Top -- Despite a Change in Leadership**. During our follow-up visit to this company, the new Chief Executive Officer (CEO) expressed concern that his corporation was still not where he wanted it to be with regard to diversity, but that they were actively attempting to monitor internal systems to ensure that qualified minorities and women could have access to the top based on merit. The company has made equal employment opportunity a performance appraisal standard for senior management and has experienced good results in expecting managers to make good faith efforts to include qualified women and minorities for promotional considerations.

*   **Reaffirmation and Commitment to Inclusivity and Diversity**. Actions include a new performance appraisal system which contains a specific component appraising performance in the area of equal opportunity and making this an integrated management concern, not just a human resource function; corporate-wide diversity training to increase management understanding of the importance of nondiscrimination and good faith efforts in hiring, promotional and management development opportunities; and implementation of an employee opinion survey to provide confidential feedback.

*   **One Company's Pipelines Yield Success**. A reorganization at this large Fortune 500 company resulted in the placement of all of the corporation's equal employment responsibility under a centralized management structure, and the establishment of critical measures to achieving workforce diversity. Since January 1, 1992,

a number of women have been appointed to senior management positions, two of whom are members of a minority group. A minority male was also appointed to a group manager position.

III. Beyond the Pilot Reviews

Compliance reviews have continued in a measured, precise fashion. Results indicate that many of the companies audited since last year have changed their culture to one which values diversity. We continue to find that if the CEO is committed to ensuring diversity, it can happen. Such commitment notwithstanding, progress varies. Examples include:

*   **A non-traditional industry for women**, a utility company in which the workforce had been primarily male for the past 100 years, is taking large strides to develop a diverse workforce through the new CEO's requirement of good faith efforts and accountability at each level of management. Actions include an executive recruitment effort which led to the hiring of women and minorities in high level positions; and the development of systems of mentoring, networking and identification of minorities and women with potential and providing them with information on career paths.

*   **A company without a formal system for development** and few women and minorities in the pipelines for advancement, agreed to work to enhance the skills of all its employees, and appointed a top management team to monitor results of diversity efforts. Additionally, this employer is taking pro-active steps to recruit minorities and women through scholarships, outreach efforts, and greater visibility in the employment community.

*   **A corporation with little emphasis on diversity** is changing the
corporate culture to one that values diversity. A reorganization and the
arrival of a new CEO from outside the corporation, have formed the
groundwork for a corporate-wide commitment to developing a diverse
workforce. The company agreed to many positive steps which include
improving the workforce participation of minorities and women,
monitoring for nondiscrimination, and ensuring that equal employment
becomes an integrated business function of the corporation.

IV.   Areas Warranting Greater Attention

Several of the barriers for women and minorities cited in the initial glass ceiling
report continue to exist in companies reviewed this year.

*   **A lack of consistent recruitment practices to attract a
diverse pool of talent.** While entry level corporate hiring is
generally well-documented, systems of recruitment and tracking
generally did not exist above a certain level.

*   **A lack of opportunity to contribute and participate in
corporate development experiences.** Another Business Week
survey, October 1991, further found that, "In regular B-school
programs -- usually paid for by the participants, not an employer --
there are plenty of women and minorities...Yet in the prestigious
programs paid for by corporations that round out a manager's
credentials at a key career point, usually at age 40 or 45,
companies are making only a token investment in developing
female and minority executives. Only about 3 percent of the 180
executives in Stanford's recent advanced-management program
were women."

*   **A general lack of corporate ownership in affirming that the practice of equal employment opportunity is an organizational responsibility, not one person's.**

Beyond those barriers, other issues have surfaced which appear to hinder the hiring and advancement of minorities and women. Some women expressed concern that they were not held to the same **performance measures** as men, and believed they had to work twice as hard. Mid level female managers in one company recently audited almost uniformly mentioned that the company was "not willing to take risks on women." These women felt they had to work twice as hard to prove they were as committed as men in the workforce, and had to stay in grade longer before promotion.

In many companies, the ability to relocate continues to be a requirement to career progression and advancement to the executive suite. The Department consistently states that if **mobility** is a requirement for career advancement, then management must also offer mobility opportunities to qualified minorities and women, ought to explain to them the benefits of acceptance, and must not make career assumptions for members of these groups.

V.   What Works

There are a number of creative and effective approaches which employers are adopting in an effort to provide access into middle and upper management positions for qualified minorities and women. Indeed, the Department has recognized with annual awards several companies which have developed and implemented such approaches.

Some of these approaches include:

*   Tracking Women and Minorities with Advancement Potential

*   Ensuring Access and Visibility

*   Ensuring a Bias-Free Workplace

*   Entering the Pipeline (Corporate Attention Toward)

Conclusion

We are more convinced than ever that this decade must be the decade of dialogue between employers, employees, the Federal Government and the private sector. Employers have a responsibility to ensure that there are no artificial barriers to advancement of qualified minorities and women in their workplace. The Department of Labor not only has the legal responsibility to ensure no such barriers exist, but must also provide assistance to aid in compliance. And, of course, employees must take personal responsibility for their own careers -- weighing personal and professional trade-offs.

It is only through greater understanding and heightened awareness to issues that true and lasting progress will occur. The Department of Labor continues to assist employers in identifying and eliminating barriers.

I. WORKFORCE TRENDS

Multicultural diversity ... managing diversity ... valuing diversity ... cultural awareness ... all of these phrases attempt to capture the reality that the workforce of tomorrow will be one very different from 10 years ago. **Workforce 2000**, a study done by the Hudson Institute Inc., for the Department of Labor in 1987, did much to heighten awareness of the demographic trends of this decade.

A recent Towers Perrin survey of 200 corporations found that 54 percent of those responding said that management support for workforce-related programs had increased over the last two years. It noted "...the single greatest factor contributing to the increase in support is senior management's heightened awareness of workforce issues and the impact those issues have on the company's profitability and competitive position."[1]

While it is encouraging to find an increased interest in diversity, the serious commitment to ensure that such diversity exists at all levels of the corporate world is not generally apparent. Progress in the advancement of qualified minorities and women into mid and senior level management positions has taken place. The success stories remain, however, the exception rather than the rule.

A Business Week survey of 400 female managers found that almost half of the respondents believe that large companies have done "somewhat better" over the last five years in hiring and promoting women executives. More than half also believe that the rate of progress has slowed down. Seventy percent of those female managers polled believe that the male-dominated corporate culture was an obstacle to their success (up from 60 percent two years ago).

---

[1] "Workforce 2000 Today: A Bottom-Line Concern," Towers Perrin, March, 1992.

Additionally, that survey found that one-third of the respondents thought that in 5 years the number of female senior executives at their companies will have either remained the same or have fallen.[2]

A recent study of career progressions of male and female managers in 20 Fortune 500 companies by researchers at Loyola University of Chicago and the Kellogg Graduate School of Management found that while these two groups of comparators were alike in almost every way, the "women with equal or better educations earn less on average than men and there are proportionately fewer women in top management positions." The study showed that female managers and professionals with similar qualifications, educational attainment, career-orientation, comparable jobs, and ability to relocate, had actually been transferred or relocated less frequently than their male colleagues (which was key to advancement), and their salaries had progressed far less rapidly over the past five years.[3] According to Loyola researcher Linda K. Stroh, the "women were not only disadvantaged but discriminated against."[4]

When the president of the New York-based executive search firm of Battalie Winston International wanted to know which of America's most senior women executives were being groomed for the top rung of the corporate ladder, she decided to call a couple hundred of them to find out. A survey of senior women executives revealed the fact that "none ... believed they would be able to overcome the barriers -- both subtle and overt -- to reach the top."[5]

---

[2] "Corporate Women. Progress? Sure. But the Playing Field is Still Far From Level," Business Week, June 8, 1992.

[3] "All the Right Stuff: A Comparison of Female and Male Managers' Career Progression," Stroh, Brett, and Reilly, October, 1991.

[4] "Corporate Women," Business Week, June 8, 1992.

[5] New York Newsday, October 20, 1991.

Other studies and articles recently released are more encouraging. In the
insurance industry, "women today believe that things have definitely changed.
By all accounts, they say the industry now offers genuine opportunities for
women in all areas -- including the technical, actuarial and investment arenas
which had typically been the domain of men."[6]

An internal Korn/Ferry study found that in 1981, five percent of its senior level
placements were women; in 1991, the figure rose to 16 percent. In 1981, none
of the women were placed in jobs at higher than vice president; last year, 21
percent were named senior vice president and above at major companies.
"There is still a pay gap there, and women are still catching up in terms of
base salary," according to Caroline W. Nahas, managing vice president and
partner of Korn/Ferry International. "Though we placed women executives in
consumer products firms, financial services and manufacturing, a higher
percentage were in health care and non-profit organizations, and they are
lower-paying industries in general," according to Nahas.[7]

---

[6]   Risk and Insurance, June, 1992.

[7]   The Washington Post, May 17, 1992.

Overall Trends in the Federal Contractor Community

To assess participation trends, the Department's Office of Federal Contract
Compliance Programs examined the "officials and managers" category in its
EEO-1 database.[8] It is important to note that the category of "officials and
managers" is so broadly defined it includes the head of clerical pools and the
janitorial services, as well as senior executives and chief executive officers.
Additionally, since these data are only for Federal contractors' workforces, they
may not always reflect changes in the labor force during similar time periods.
An example is the large increase in total U.S. payroll employment -- almost 18
million between 1981 and 1991 -- and a decrease in Federal contractors'
workforces during the same time period.

Comparisons among the approximately 90,000 Federal contractors reporting
establishments showed that between 1981 and 1991 the total number of
employees had decreased by 4.7 million. There was an increase, however, in
both the number and percentage of minorities and women who are employed
by these companies as officials and managers.

In 1981, there were 246,503 minority officials and managers. By 1991, this
number had grown to 264,449, an increase of 7.3 percent. The proportion of
officials and managers who were minorities increased slightly from 8 percent in
1981 to 10 percent in 1991. Comparable data for women showed an increase
of 12 percent. The proportion of officials and managers who were women
increased from 18 percent in 1981 to 25 percent in 1991.

---

[8] EEO-1 data are drawn from Employer Information Reports that are submitted
each year by Federal contractors with 50 or more employees and a contract for
$50,000 or more.

Percent of Officials and Managers Who Were Minorities and Women

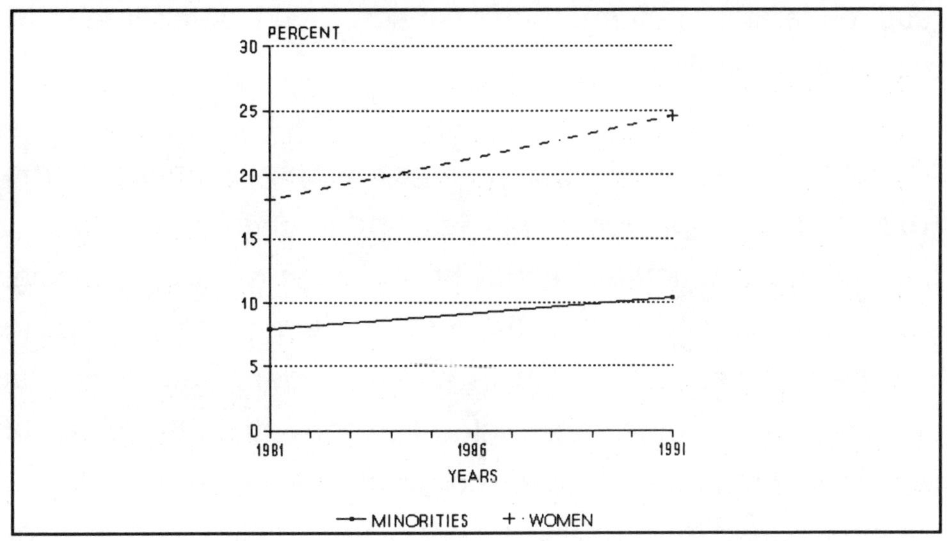

A.   Major Industries

In 1981, nearly 44 percent of all minority officials and managers were
employed in retail trade, finance and real estate, and durable manufacturing.
Members of minority groups comprised more than 10 percent of the officials
and managers in retail trade, other services, and communications industries,
and more than 13 percent of the officials and managers in the health services.

By 1991, this picture had changed slightly with nondurable manufacturing
replacing retail trade as one of the top three industries. Slightly less than 43
percent of all minority officials and managers were in these top industries.
This slight shift in industry concentration indicates that minority officials and
managers were more dispersed throughout the other industry categories. In
1991, minorities represented more than 10 percent of the total number of
officials and managers in five industrial groups. The proportion was again

highest in health services at 15 percent, followed by communications at 13 percent, retail trade at 12 percent, other services at 11 percent, and finance and real estate at 10 percent.

Several differences were found when changes in employment patterns between 1981 and 1991 for women officials and managers were analyzed. In 1981, the top three industries employing the most women as officials and managers were finance and real estate, retail trade, and communications. Nearly 53 percent of the women officials and managers were employed in these three industries. Women accounted for more than 33 percent of the officials and managers in finance and real estate, retail trade, and communications industries, and 58 percent of the officials and managers in health services.

Minority women represented 4 percent to 8 percent of the officials and managers in these industries. Women were less than 10 percent of the officials and managers in wholesale trade, transportation, machinery manufacturing and durable manufacturing, but there was no industry group where women were fewer than 5 percent of the officials and managers.

By 1991, the employment patterns of women officials and managers had also changed. Nondurable manufacturing replaced retail trade in the top three industries. The number of women who were officials and managers in the top three industries decreased slightly to 310,137, or 49 percent, of all women who were officials and managers. Since the total number of women who were officials and managers grew by 12 percent between 1981 and 1991, this decrease indicates a greater dispersion among all industry categories.

Indeed by 1991, there were no major industry categories where the participation of women was less than 10 percent in the officials and managers category. The proportion of women officials and managers was greatest in the same four industries as in 1981, growing to more than 40 percent in each, with the proportion in health services increasing to 64 percent. The proportion of minority women in these industries ranged from a low of six percent of the officials and managers in retail sales to 10 percent in health services.

B.   Large Companies

Comparisons were made between the top 100 Fortune 500 companies that were Federal contractors in 1991 and smaller Federal contractors (those with 500 to 1,000 employees). For both groups, the number and proportion of women and minorities who were officials and managers increased between 1981 and 1991. However, the proportion of women and minorities who were officials and managers was greater in the smaller establishments each year.

In 1991, for example, women were 25 percent of the officials and managers in smaller establishments compared to 18 percent in the top 100 Fortune 500 companies. Minorities were 10 percent of the officials and managers in the smaller establishments. African Americans were 5 percent of this group; Hispanics, 3 percent; Asians, 2 percent; and Native Americans, less than 1 percent. Minorities were 7 percent of the officials and managers in the top 100 Fortune 500 companies. Of this group, African Americans were 3 percent; Hispanics and Asians, 2 percent each; and Native Americans were less than 1 percent.

The percent change between 1981 and 1991 for minority officials and managers in the top 100 was 49 percent. Officials and managers in smaller establishments increased 18 percent. The changes for women were 103 percent for the top 100. With the exception of Native Americans, each group of minority women increased its number by more than 100 percent between 1981 and 1991. The change for all women for the smaller establishments was 34 percent.

II. CORPORATE MANAGEMENT (GLASS CEILING) REVIEWS

The Department of Labor's pilot reviews completed in 1991, assisted the Department in developing guidance for the conduct of future reviews. Additionally, they helped the Department identify barriers to the advancement of qualified minorities and women.

While many of the contractors in the pilot reviews signed agreements to correct deficiencies found, it was the Department's responsibility to monitor progress -- and at times revisit -- these companies to ensure that corrective actions had, in fact, taken place.

The following are results from three examples out of our pilot reviews where OFCCP undertook corporate progress reports, and follow-up visits.

A. Commitment Continues at the Top -- Despite a Change in Leadership

One company from the pilot study underwent a change in leadership in the highest ranks since the review was closed last year. Keeping in line with the company's preference for growing its own internal workforce talent, the recently appointed CEO had more than 35 years of experience with the company.

During our follow-up visit with the new leadership, the new CEO reaffirmed his company's commitment to a diverse and well-qualified workforce. He stated he was committed to ensuring that he had a well-trained and diverse workforce. He was concerned that his corporation was still not where he wanted it to be with regard to equal employment opportunity, but that they actively were attempting to monitor internal systems to ensure that qualified minorities and women could have access to the top based on merit. Additionally, any barriers identified would be removed.

The actions of this company matched the Chief Executive Officer's words. Our follow-up visit identified numerous promotions and other positive steps toward managing a diverse workforce. Since the pilot review of over a year ago, the company has made equal employment opportunity a performance appraisal standard for senior management and has experienced progress in seeing that managers make good faith efforts to include qualified minorities and women for promotional considerations.   An internal task force on the development and promotion of women met during the year and made recommendations to the senior executives of the company. Several women were promoted during the year, with one acquiring "Officer" status. The company was also more actively monitoring total compensation packages for nondiscrimination.

The corporate executives reaffirmed their commitment to ensure that minorities and women had access to line management positions, and detailed progress made in the area of equal employment opportunity, both within the U.S. and on international assignments. The corporate-wide system of transfers and placements has become an area with greater oversight to ensure nondiscrimination. Ensuring that qualified minorities and women have access to these opportunities is now a corporate management responsibility. The company's executives also committed themselves to take good faith efforts to bring qualified minorities into the feeder positions in the company.

B.   Reaffirmation and Commitment to Inclusivity and Diversity

At the time of the pilot review, a Fortune 500 company was in a state of transition with regard to equal employment monitoring and accountability. The departure of its expert on EEO matters, and the organizational dynamics caused by a change in corporate leadership, had brought to a standstill this company's systems of internal control and accountability which previously had been in place.   Several years earlier, this company had implemented systems to monitor and remedy exclusionary practices. At the time of the Department's pilot review, all formal systems announcing job opportunities within the company had ceased, as well as the monitoring of hiring, development, promotion, and turnover. As a result of the review last year, the company agreed to remedy violations and problem areas identified during the audit.

During a follow-up visit by Department officials, the company shared with the Department corrective measures it undertook to meet its commitment. These included:

- Implementation of a new corporate-wide performance appraisal system which includes a specific component appraising performance in the area of equal employment opportunity, making this an integrated management concern, not just a human resource function. (At the time of the initial glass ceiling review, performance appraisals were very subjective, and the company had a policy of grooming one's own successor. Neither of these practices was being monitored.)

- Institution of corporate-wide diversity training to increase management's understanding of the importance of nondiscrimination and making good faith efforts in hiring, promotional and management development opportunities.

- Promotion or hiring of several minorities and women in mid and upper level corporate management positions.

- Implementation of a new employee opinion survey to allow employees to provide confidential feedback on areas of concern.

- Requirement by the CEO that the human resource staff take ownership to manage internal grievances, human resource planning, training and compensation, and report results directly to him.

C.   Company With Rapid Growth through Acquisitions

This company was revisited by senior Departmental staff because of its rapid growth through acquisitions, and its prior difficulties in recruiting minorities and women.

As part of its competitive strategy, this company continues to operate with a lean management staff. Its workforce has been very stable over the past year, with little turnover, and employment expansion has been through the purchase of other companies and their workforces. As a result, almost a year after signing an agreement with the Department to correct problem areas, there were no notable workforce changes in the company, although the company implemented the commitments contained in the agreement with the Department.

This company has poor participation of minorities and women at all levels of management and in some professional ranks. While the company prefers an informal system of recruitment, via word-of-mouth, networking, etc., it is now well aware of its legal responsibilities not only to keep records, but also to monitor corporate practices to ensure they do not exclude qualified minorities and women.

The company continues to have programs for the development, and increased visibility of qualified high potential employees in the corporate pipelines. While there does not appear to be any immediate opportunity for management advancement for these individuals, these programs do provide readiness support and credential-building opportunities, and are being treated in that fashion. This example is similar to many companies that are streamlining their management ranks and flattening the corporate structure.

D.   One Company's Pipelines Yield Success

Another Fortune 500 company which was reviewed in the pilot study has made significant progress. A reorganization to place all of the corporation's responsibilities for equal employment opportunity under a single well-integrated human resource management structure has taken place.

After the review, the company established critical success factors which could be charted and measured, incorporating a strategic plan devoted to the achievement of workforce diversity. Among these initiatives were:

- Awarding grants to 33 high schools to support math and science courses.

- Scheduling a diversity conference involving senior management.

- Developing a strategic plan managed by the Senior Vice President for Human Resources.

- Conducting a diversity planning session which included personnel directors from each business unit. This session finalized a three-year diversity implementation plan to measure progress through 1995. With input from each business unit, six core groups were established for planning and designing the factors to achieve the strategic thrust, and reporting results to an executive/senior management steering committee. These efforts include education of management in glass ceiling issues and regular department-head meetings within each business unit with that unit's president and his/her direct reports to measure progress.

The advancement of minorities and women can already be seen at this company. Since January 1, 1992, a number of well-qualified women have been appointed to senior management positions, two of whom are members of a minority group. In addition, a minority male was appointed to a group manager position. It is also noteworthy that the president of a major operating company is a woman, and during the fourth quarter of 1991 that same unit hired a woman as senior vice president for marketing.

III. BEYOND THE PILOT STUDIES

As part of the Department's comprehensive glass ceiling program, additional companies have been audited for glass ceiling issues, or are involved in the audit process as this report goes to print.

As in the pilot reviews, corporate management reviews differ from other reviews in the level of sophistication necessary to conduct them, the in-depth analyses of corporate policies and practices affecting senior management selection decisions, and the close oversight by senior level Departmental staff.

A.   Corporation in a Non-Traditional Industry

Another company audited for glass ceiling compliance was a utility company that provides electric and natural gas service to a major U.S. city. This company historically has valued individuals working hard at the entry level, working their way up the career ladder -- from meter reader to senior executive. The workforce had been primarily male over the past 100 years. The review validated the corporation's cultural bias toward longevity and hard work---almost all of the senior executives were found to have come up through the company's ranks. The company has a very stable workforce with an extremely low turnover rate.

Over the last five years, with the emergence of a new CEO, this company has taken significant strides to develop a diverse workforce. Specifically, the CEO required that good faith efforts be taken at each of the divisions of the company, placing final accountability with the top level managers of these divisions. The accountability was then passed down to each level of management within the divisions, and did not become the responsibility of only one person or of the human resources office.

The Department's review of this public utility company found that: a) while minorities are currently employed at a level lower than females, there was no discrimination or artificial impediment to their advancement; b) while women and minorities were not well represented in the top level positions, in most instances when vacancies occurred, positive steps had been taken to identify qualified minority and female candidates; and, c) the company was not adequately monitoring all compensation programs, succession planning and promotion programs.

Problem areas were discussed and the company took appropriate corrective action. Moreover, this company took the initiative to develop a plan which would give management exposure to its minorities and women. Specifically, the company developed an Equal Opportunity Task Force to monitor selection decisions, discuss EEO concerns with managers and to attempt to resolve other issues. Executive recruitment efforts led to the hiring of women and minorities in high-level positions. The company also developed systems of mentoring, networking, and identifying minorities and women with potential and providing them with information on career paths. In addition, employees, including minorities and women, were assigned to special projects which provided visibility and promotional potential.

With the positive steps that the contractor is taking to diversify the workplace, it is expected that a pool of qualified candidates will be available for mid and upper level management positions, as vacancies occur.

B.   A Large Employer With Many Management Opportunities

This employer is an established, 75-year-old company of substantial size. The company has a broad product mix, has maintained an overall progressive employment record, and has been, except for one or two periods, highly profitable.

The corporation, with several thousand managers, regularly reviews its employment practices affecting minorities and women.

The participation rate of minorities and women in the corporate office, where several hundred officials are employed, is better than many other similarly situated companies. Almost one-third are women or minorities, although most are in lower management positions. A woman currently holds a "line" (technical) vice presidency.

While female and minority representation is not uniform at all management levels, real progress is occurring. Furthermore, no disparity based on gender or minority status in salaries, benefits, evaluations, retention, or turnover has been identified.

Further, the company has a system which identifies high-potential employees at all levels and affords such persons special opportunities for task force and committee assignments, rotations, and further education.

New college graduates, after a year of employment, are evaluated for possible selection into a high-potential development program. Over 900 such employees are currently in the program, with 30 to 35 selected from the corporate office each year. Women are well represented, as are, but to a lesser extent, minorities.

For mid level managers, a less formalized program identifies high-potential employees, and keys them to career paths, identifying jobs to which they might advance as vacancies occur. Minorities and women are well represented in this program.

Finally, a high level succession plan, administered by the CEO, addresses executive positions and identifies some 100 individuals with high-potentials for top leadership roles.

As a means of monitoring the participation and treatment of minorities and women in these plans, executive level managers have applicable standards included in their annual appraisals. In addition, the CEO receives regular reports concerning the representation and status of high-potential minorities and women.

Given the formalized tracking of its high-potential employees, the non-biased evaluation and compensation system in place, and the strong commitment expressed by the CEO and other executives to equal employment and upward mobility opportunities for minorities and women, the pipeline is one which should produce increased diversity in the executive suite.

C.   Corporation with Little Formality

Many Fortune 500 corporations have highly structured systems for tracking applicants, and developing key contributors, those they believe are high-potential, or those deemed promotable. Other companies still have more loosely defined systems, or no systems at all.

A recently audited company is listed as a Fortune 500 company because of its large volume of sales. Its culture is one of openness and informality. There were no formal systems for development, promotion, special assignments or projects.   As with many other companies the Department audits, this company preferred to "grow its own" employees, utilizing the internal pipelines for most promotions (and the few transfers made from corporate establishments). The review validated that most employees at the highest ranks had many years with the company. "Length of service, hard work, and dedication" were the values the company rewarded.

The highest-ranked minority and the highest ranked woman were at the same reporting level to the CEO. The minority was in a traditional staff function; the woman was in a line position with input into the company's bottom line profitability.   While women tended to plateau in the lowest supervisory levels, minorities capped-out well before reaching even entry level management positions.

The majority of the company's deficiencies, for which they were cited, concerned issues of outreach and good faith efforts in hiring minorities and women into the pipelines. In fact, the company appeared to have no impediments to advancement. The problem was getting into the pipelines because the company had a relatively small pool of women and a general absence of minorities.

As a result of this audit, the company agreed to:

- Establish a top management team to monitor results of diversity efforts, monitor positions in the pipeline, monitor salary increases, bonuses and promotions, and ensure enhanced manager and supervisory EEO training and staff development.

- Enhance the skills of all employees, including minorities and women, to take advantage of the development opportunities.

- Establish three scholarship programs for: inner-city at-risk youth; a school of business scholarship; and a chemical engineering scholarship at a historically African American college or university, in an effort to become more involved with, and part of, communities that will channel a more diverse talent pool to this company.

D.   New and Emerging Companies: Work on the Ground Floor

This is a high tech company in a competitive, relatively new field that enjoyed phenomenal growth since its creation. Further, it has a highly organized employee evaluation, development and reward system.

Although this company employs a large numbers of electrical engineers, many with advanced degrees, this company has difficulty finding a diverse pool of candidates for employment. It has a substantial number of professionals of Asian heritage, yet relatively few African Americans, Hispanics, or women in either management or mid level professional ranks.

While there are not large numbers of women and certain minority groups obtaining technological degrees, minorities with engineering degrees are being hired by this company at the same rate as minorities graduating from engineering schools. The company, however, has undertaken a vigorous college recruitment program, including summer internships and cooperative work-study programs. In recent years, over half of the entry level administrative vacancies filled by new college graduates with bachelors degrees were women. Of recent graduates placed in technical (scientific) positions, nearly one-fifth were women.

Up to the time of the review, only 30 to 40 percent of all entry level exempt positions were filled by new college graduates. The remainder came from employee referrals (where a bonus is given to those employees successfully referring an applicant), from networking and from recruitment firms. No discrimination was identified as a result of these latter approaches. But neither did this system contribute to expanding the participation of women and minorities. Rather, it has served to promote the status quo.

During the review, the company, realizing that its well-developed college recruitment program and summer internships brought in a cadre of qualified minorities and women, agreed to expand the number of positions offered through these vehicles.

With the pipeline opening, this contractor is ideally poised to assure the future progress of minorities and women.

What makes this company unique is the sophisticated evaluation system it has developed. This should assure that high-potential minorities and women who possess outstanding qualifications will be identified and advanced.

The company's evaluation system not only critically appraises all of its employees on a regular basis, but it also ranks them within their respective work groups, and measures their development trend in comparison with their peers. Frequent personal development appraisals allow individual employees to plan their own career growth, including opportunities available for work-related educational programs, and rotational or permanent reassignments. Identification of key employees, high potentials, and other designations rise directly from these evaluation systems.

A review of recent employee evaluations, rankings, trend patterns, retention, salaries, bonuses, stock options, turnover and retention rates showed no adverse disparity against minorities or women.

Thus, while the current participation rate of minorities and women in middle and upper management jobs is minimal, the pipelines are opening, and, more importantly, a system is in place and is being judiciously administered to assure advancement into all levels based on competence and desire.

E.   Changing a Corporate Culture to One of Diversity

The Department audited a corporation located in a major urban city. Sitting comfortably in the upper third of the Fortune 500 list, this company has faced and survived (within the past five years) substantial financial, legal, and organizational challenges. Although the company survived, the resulting reorganization left the corporation with a workforce of about one-half its original size. During this period of stress and organizational upheaval, equal employment opportunity was not a primary corporate concern, or, even secondary, as our review discovered.

The new CEO, the first to be brought in from outside the organization, quickly announced concern at the current EEO profile and expressed commitment to workforce diversity and to utilize the full potential of each employee.

While this has lent encouragement to the women and minorities occupying lower and mid level management positions, it has caused some consternation among those for whom, in the past, longevity and tenure were a key component to advancement. The CEO established three priorities to ensure the success and growth of the organization: 1) Customer Satisfaction; 2) Shareholder Value, and 3) Individual Dignity -- recognizing the value of each employee which will make the company the preferred place of employment.

As it is located in a "rust belt" city with a declining industrial base, the company has contended, with certain justification, that it is difficult to attract and retain talented minorities and women, especially those unmarried and/or just graduating from college. This said, the last year or two of college recruitment efforts have resulted in an excellent group of female hires, both minority and non-minority. The company's inability to attract minority males was unexplained, and it was not possible to audit their good faith recruitment efforts due to lack of adequate recordkeeping. While the participation of minorities and women was never exceptionally high, many in the pipeline were lost over the last five years.

One of the casualties of the reorganization and restructuring was the neglect of recordkeeping and subsequent monitoring of EEO activities. This deficiency made the OFCCP audit task especially difficult. A primary result of the OFCCP compliance review was the institution of a comprehensive EEO audit and reporting system which will enable the corporate management to identify areas of EEO concern and initiate corrective action. Within the past two years the company has instituted a formalized executive development and succession planning program.

On the positive side, even prior to the OFCCP review, the company had taken some steps on its own to attract and retain high-potential minorities and women.   For example, a slate of candidates produced by an executive search firm was rejected by the corporation for failing to include qualified minorities for consideration.

This company has made continuous progress under strong EEO management since the initial glass ceiling review was completed. Actual results are now being realized through increased representation of females and minorities at higher levels of the corporation -- the pipelines to the top.

By the time this review had concluded, the company had taken several additional positive steps to improve access of minorities and women into its senior level management ranks. One woman was promoted from a mid level to a senior level position. The company recruited externally and hired a minority woman for a position as a corporate vice president. Additionally, for the first time in the company's history, it promoted a woman to a plant manager position.

IV.   AREAS WARRANTING GREATER ATTENTION

The Report on the Glass Ceiling Initiative cited the following as barriers to career advancement:

A.   **Recruitment Practices** -- Although entry level corporate hiring is generally well-documented, consistent recruitment and tracking practices generally did not exist above a certain level. A commitment to make good faith efforts to attract a broad, diverse pool of talent from which to hire was not apparent.

B.   **Lack of Opportunity to Contribute and Participate in Corporate Development Experiences** -- Often elaborate corporate systems of early identification, career development, needs assessments, and succession planning were not monitored to ensure access for qualified minorities and women.

C.   **General Lack of Corporate Ownership of Equal Opportunity Principles** -- When Departmental staff discussed diversity and a commitment to take appropriate good faith measures, managers often expressed that such responsibilities were someone else's -- the human resources division's, or the EEO Director -- but not their's.

These barriers continued to be evident in additional reviews performed by the Department. Corporate hiring practices -- whether informal word-of-mouth referrals, or employee referral systems that do not look to a diverse pool of applicants -- continued to be cited as violations of the Department's mandates of good faith efforts in hiring, and were remedied by the companies reviewed.

It warrants noting that during compliance audits, the Department continues to find areas of the corporate workforce, or complete industries, that do not have a diverse workforce. This may be due, in part, to the relatively small number of minorities and women with the necessary educational attainments -- receiving degrees (both bachelors and advanced) in math and the sciences for example. Specifically, according to a report by the American Association of University Women Educational Foundation, "girls who are highly competent in math and science are much less likely to pursue scientific or technological careers than their class mates."[9] There has also been a marked drop (11.1%) in the number of women receiving bachelors degrees in engineering over the past five years. There has, however, been an increase in the number of African Americans receiving such degrees (9.0%), and an even greater increase in the number of Native American Indians (13.2%), Hispanics (19.6%), and Asians (30.6%).[10]

The inclusion of qualified minorities and women in all corporate developmental systems and practices continues to be an area of close scrutiny by the Department. Executive development, developmental experiences paid for by corporate America, does not appear to be provided as often to minorities and women.

A Business Week survey of October 1991, found that corporate America invests billions of dollars in executive-education programs as an important step in "fast track" managers' development. For minorities and women, this survey, nonetheless, presents a mixed set of findings. Perhaps Business Week said it

---

[9] The American Association of University Women Educational Foundation Report, "How Schools Shortchange Girls," 1992.

[10] Engineering Manpower Commission, 1992.

best: "In regular B-school programs -- usually paid for by the participant, not an employer -- there are plenty of women and minorities. ... Yet in the prestigious programs paid for by corporations that round out a manager's credentials at a key career point, usually at age 40 or 45, companies are making only a token investment in developing female and minority executives. A case in point: Only about 3 percent of the 180 executives in Stanford's recent advanced-management program were women. ...There is only one real explanation, and it is a damning one: Many big corporations simply aren't committed to helping women and minorities to the executive suite."[11]

Ensuring that corporate practices involving management development, credential-building experiences, and special assignments be carried out in a nondiscriminatory manner is an important responsibility of the Department's corporate audit program.

While these practices can become barriers and will continue to be closely monitored, other issues have surfaced that warrant inclusion in this report. Such issues may pose barriers to some individuals and in some companies.

1.   **Performance Measures:** Many women expressed concern to representatives of the Department that they were not held to the same performance measures as men and believed they had to work twice as hard. Mid level female managers in one company recently audited almost uniformly mentioned that the company was "not willing to take risks on women." These women felt they had to work twice as hard to prove they were as committed as men in the workforce, and had to stay in grade longer before promotion. In companies with informal appraisal systems, monitoring to ensure that minorities and women are being held to the same performance measures is even more difficult.

---

[11] Business Week, October 28, 1991.

**   "Men seem to be promoted on their potential. Women get promoted on their performance, and it takes longer."[12]

2.   **Mobility:** In many companies, the ability to relocate continues to be a requirement to career progression and advancement to the executive suite. This continues to be an area mentioned in focus groups, conferences and employer meetings. The Department consistently states that if mobility is a requirement for career advancement, management must offer such positions to qualified minorities and women, explain to them the benefits of acceptance, and must not make assumptions for members of these groups.

During the past year, the Department has met with individuals whose employers have done just that. An example is a female MBA graduate who was counselled by corporate management that the best career choice for her would be to accept a position with that company in a rural setting with the company's largest workforce population. She accepted the position because of the positive career implications -- the company explained that within a certain time frame she would be relocated to another establishment at a higher level.

---

[12] New York Newsday, October 20, 1991.

V.   WHAT WORKS

Beyond the issues discussed earlier, there are a number of creative and effective approaches which employers are adopting in an effort to provide advancement opportunities for minorities and women into middle and upper management.

A. Tracking Women and Minorities with Advancement Potential.

As more and more women and minorities fill entry level management positions, identifying those with high potential and tracking their progress is key to a successful effort to break the glass ceiling. Southern Bell of Georgia, for instance, received the Department's Exemplary Voluntary Effort (EVE) award last year for the company's High Potential Development Program, which has, since its inception, included minorities and women. The company has taken great care to assure that high potential individuals are not overlooked when promotional opportunities occur. A similar award was received by Tenneco, Inc. of Houston, TX, for its Integrated Leadership Initiatives program, which is designed to enhance the participation of minorities and women in corporate management positions. Several companies have made their human resources departments responsible for tracking high potential minorities and women, and reporting their status directly to the Chief Executive Officer. By thus "empowering" the human resource departments, historic functional or organizational bias within operating units is checked.

B.   Ensuring Access and Visibility.

Employers have long recognized that new managers require developmental opportunities if they are to succeed. Many companies have described their efforts to assure such opportunities are equally available to qualified minorities and women. An award was presented to the Anheuser-Busch Company of St. Louis, MO, last year for its management development programs. One involves wholesaler practices where individuals progress from positions as inventory analysts, to coordinators, to plant inventory management supervisors. The other program is in a small-scale brewery. This management development plan, designed to accomplish research in brewing and also serve as a training ground, leads to positions as brewing supervisors or supervisory trainees. Other companies have developed carefully managed programs to identify educational or experience needs among its lower level managers, and afford opportunities for development in both areas. Such companies have carefully monitored their educational grants, rotational assignments, task force and committee opportunities and other developmental programs to assure minorities and women are treated with absolute equality.

C.   Ensuring a Bias-Free Workplace.

Many companies have recognized the need to assure that any behavioral biases which may exist against women or minority not be practiced in the workplace. First, a large number of employers have been energetic in their efforts to eliminate such prejudice through clearly communicated corporate policy statements, diversity training, and swift discipline against those employees who violate company rules. Tenneco, for instance, has adopted a vigorous women's and multi-cultural advisory council, and a company-wide awareness program on workforce diversity. Other companies have undertaken employee surveys to better identify workplace attitudes that may be impeding advancement of minority group members or women. Smaller companies can also do their part. Jones Plastics and Engineering Corporation of Jeffersontown, KY, has undertaken manager and supervisor training, including situational approaches and role playing to increase sensitivity to work and family issues and policies.

D. Entering the Pipeline.

Although this report primarily addresses issues involving advancement into mid and upper level management, no long-term progress will be made in this area without continued efforts to improve placement of minorities and women into entry level professional positions. The Department's experiences find this particularly true for those companies that hire a large proportion of professionals requiring technical and scientific degrees. The efforts undertaken by many companies in this regard are also encouraging. Consolidated Diesel Company, of Whitakers, NC, for instance, received recognition for its leadership, support and financial resources to better prepare students for the work place, striving to improve educational excellence in their community. The Jet Propulsion Laboratory, of Pasadena, CA, was similarly recognized for its program of research grants, scholarships, fellowships, summer employment and collaborative research projects through historically African American colleges and universities, two universities with a high enrollment of Hispanics, and for a unique Native American initiative. The Native American effort supports students studying science and engineering, and places a special emphasis on family involvement, and community and tribal leadership in supporting and motivating the students. At Johns Hopkins University's Applied Physics Laboratory in Laurel, MD, the employer has spearheaded a consortium that enabled more than 700 students to receive engineering master's degrees.

CONCLUSION

As we prepare for the 21st century we must develop a well-trained, skilled, professional and productive workforce that will be globally competitive. This must be done with a workforce that is inclusive and supports diversity ... where human talent is not excluded for any reason as unrelated to ability as sex, race, religion, national origin, disability, or veteran status.

The release of the Department of Labor's Report on the Glass Ceiling Initiative (August, 1991), not only established a benchmark for measuring progress, but also stimulated much action toward discussing and identifying artificial barriers to advancement (glass ceilings). As a result of our concerted efforts over the last two years, we are more convinced than ever that each and every one of us has an important role to play in this issue.

- All employers have an economic, demographic, social, and moral responsibility to ensure that no artificial barriers to advancement of qualified minorities and women exist in their companies.

- As the only agency that can pro-actively audit companies for compliance (outside the filing of formal complaints), the Department of Labor has the legal responsibility to ensure that no such barriers exist. The Department has committed itself and many of its resources to cooperative compliance and technical assistance outside the formal audit setting.

- Employees too must take personal responsibilities for their own career progress. Oftentimes workplace advancement means relocating to less than ideal localities; working long hours; taking career risks; volunteering for additional assignments; or simply moving to another division -- all factors that employees must weigh, and about which they must make personal and professional decisions.

The Department stands ready to assist employers -- no matter how large or small -- in identifying and eliminating barriers to the advancement of qualified individuals in their workplace, and to assist in educating employees of their personal responsibilities as well. And, we will fully, firmly, and fairly enforce the laws we have been entrusted to enforce.

In 1935 Margaret Mead wrote, "If we are to achieve a richer culture, rich in contrasting values, we must recognize the whole gamut of human potentialities." It is our hope that "Pipelines of Progress" serves as another tool to reach that higher plane.

*U.S. Government Printing Office: 1992 — 312-412/74354